CONTENTS

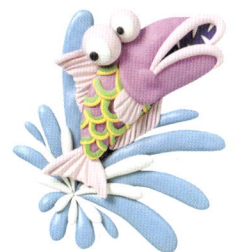

When It Comes to
Bugs

A poem to share

Written by Aileen Fisher
Illustrated by Clive Taylor

I like crawlers,
I like creepers,
hoppers, jumpers,
fliers, leapers,
walkers, stalkers,
chirpers, peepers...

3

I wonder why
my mother thinks
that finders
can't be keepers.

4

Cobweb

Written by Marion Rego
Illustrated by Nicolas van Pallandt

6

In our garage,
a spider makes
a cobweb.
It goes in and out,
around and around.
Every morning,
the cobweb is there.

In the morning,
we run to the car.

"Come on, Mum!"
we say.
"We are late!"

Mum comes out
and runs into the web.

"Oh no, not again!"
she says.

"The cobweb is there
every morning," we say.
"Now the spider
has to make
another one."

"That spider has
to learn to make
a cobweb in another
place," says Mum.

But the spider
goes in and out,
around and around.
It makes
another cobweb
in the same place.

15

In the morning,
Mum runs
into the new cobweb.

"That spider has
to learn," she says.

"She's done it again!"
we say.
"Mum has to learn, too!"

17

Moth

Written by Dawn McMillan
Illustrated by Christine Ross

18

Tap! Tap! Tap!
Something was
at the window.
It was Moth.

"Let me in!" said Moth.
"Let me into the light."

Simon's family
looked up
at the window.

"No! No!" shouted Mum.

"No! No!" shouted Dad.

"No! No!" shouted
Aunt May.

"Yes!" said Simon.
He opened
the window.

In flew Moth –
past Simon's face,
around Mum's book,
over Dad's paper,
and into
Aunt May's hair!

"Help!" shouted
Aunt May.

Moth fell to the floor.

"I will put Moth
in a jar," said Simon.

Simon looked at Moth.
Mum looked at Moth.
Dad looked at Moth.
Aunt May
looked at Moth.

31

"I think Moth wants
to get out," said Simon.

"Yes," said Mum.

"Yes," said Dad.

"Yes," said Aunt May.
"Take Moth outside
and set it free."

So Simon did!

Mine!

Written by Dot Meharry
Illustrated by Clive Taylor

The fly flew
over the river.

"Mmm," said the fish
when he saw the fly.
"Mine!"

37

"Mmm," said the bird when she saw the fish. "Mine!"

"Mmm," said the fox
when he saw the bird.
"Mine!"

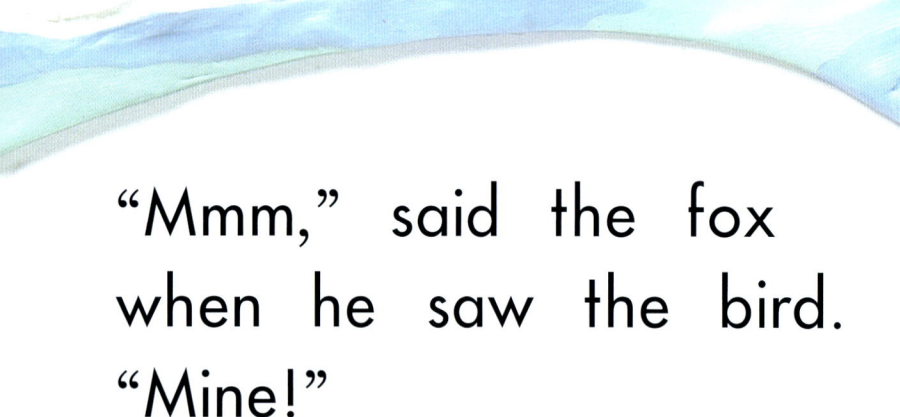

The fish jumped up,
but missed the fly.

The bird dived in,
but missed the fish.

45

The fox jumped out,
but missed the bird.

The fly flew
over the river.

"Mmm," said the spider.
"Mine!"